Union Public Library

Historical Atlases of South Asia,
Central Asia, and the Middle East™

A HISTORICAL ATLAS OF

SYRIA

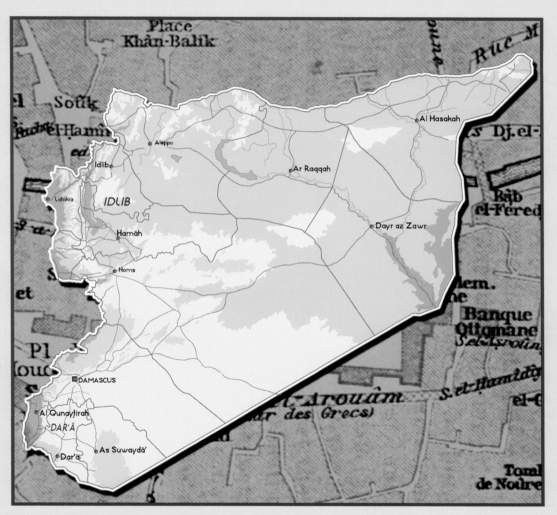

Allison Stark Draper

The Rosen Publishing Group, Inc., New York

Published in 2004 by The Rosen Publishing Group, Inc.
29 East 21st Street, New York, NY 10010

Copyright © 2004 by The Rosen Publishing Group, Inc.

First Edition

Publisher's Cataloging Data

Draper, Allison Stark
A historical atlas of Syria / Allison Stark Draper.
        p. cm.—(Historical atlases of South Asia, Central Asia, and the Middle East)
Includes bibliographical references and index.
Summary: Maps and text chronicle the history of this Middle Eastern country that is at the eastern end of the Mediterranean Sea.
ISBN 0-8239-3983-9
1. Syria—History—Maps for children 2. Syria—Maps for children [1. Syria—History
2. Atlases] I. Title II. Series
911'.5691—dc21

J
915.691
DRA
c.1

Manufactured in the United States of America

Cover images: Syria and its capital, Damascus *(current/twentieth-century maps, center)*; a statue of a shepherd *(bottom left)*; Süleyman the Magnificent *(bottom right)*; and Syria's current president, Bashar Assad *(top left)*.

Contents

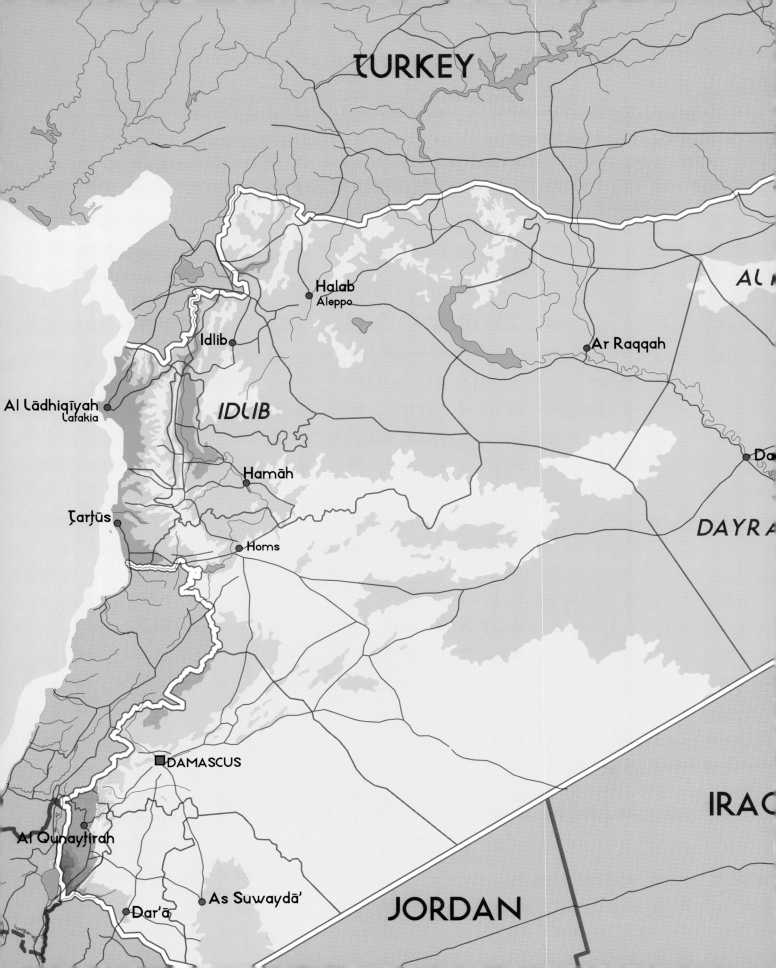

Al Hasakah

ASAKAH

az Zawr

ZAWR

INTRODUCTION

Syria is an ancient land. For four thousand years, it has stood as a gateway between Asia and the Western world. Damascus, Syria's capital, is thought to be the oldest continuously inhabited city in the world. The country's great history is due to its geography. Set at the eastern end of the Mediterranean Sea, south of Turkey, northeast of Israel, north of Jordan, and west of Iraq and Iran, Syria is at the heart of the Middle East. Its land has always been strategically valuable because of its position. The Romans conquered Syria to bridge their way to the East. The Arabs made it their capital when they emerged from the wilderness of the Arabian Peninsula. The Turks later used Syria to link themselves with Palestine and Egypt. In the twentieth century, the French occupied Syria for its political and trade value.

Syria's history is not only one of invasion. Centuries before Alexander the Great

Over the centuries, Syria, as well as its capital city of Damascus, have been home to Roman, Greek, Arab, and Turkish empires. Governed by the French after the decline of the Ottoman Empire during World War I (1914–1918), Syria first gained independence as a nation in 1946. In the 1967 Arab-Israeli War, Syria lost the Golan Heights to Israel. Since that time, peace talks between the two nations have been ongoing over the disputed territory.

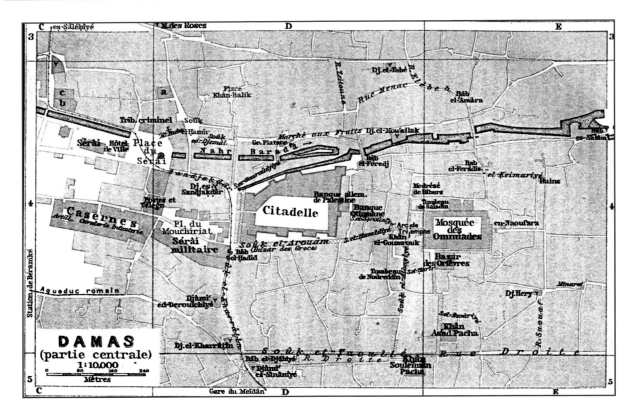

This historic map of Damascus, drawn for the French government in 1912 just before World War I, was created about the same time that British and French forces made their presence known in the region. The city itself has been a part of countless empires since the time of the Egyptians and is sometimes referred to as the world's most continuously occupied city. This map shows the Citadelle (Citadel) built by the Romans in 1219 and the Great Mosque—once a Christian church under the Romans and later an Islamic house of worship when Damascus was a capital of the Arab Empire during the mid-600s.

arrived in the fourth century BC on his way to conquer Persia, the Phoenicians of Syria had already produced an alphabet, a navy capable of crossing the Mediterranean Sea, and an early form of monotheism, a religion that preached the existence of only one god.

By the Middle Ages, Syria had pushed out its Greek and Roman conquerors and had become the center of an Arab empire that stretched from India to Spain. It housed the caliphs, who spread the religion of Islam, and

the Arab armies that drove Europe's Christian crusaders out of the East.

During the sixteenth century, Syria fell to the Ottoman Turks, an occupation that remained in place for four hundred years. By the end of World War I, with the help of England and France, the Syrians won their freedom from the Turks. However, it took another quarter century for them to rid themselves of the French. Finally, in 1946, the Syrian Arab Republic became the independent nation that it is today.

1 ANCIENT SYRIA

The birth of Syria was a slow process. For millennia, the area that would become Syria was a nameless wasteland. Geographically, the Syro-Mesopotamian desert is part of Arabia. At one time, it linked the Arabian and the Sahara Deserts with the Gobi Desert of central Asia. Unlike Arabia's desert, most of which is too dry to support life, much of Syria is not desert at all, but steppe, or semiarid plains.

The Egyptians and the Sumerians

For several centuries, the people who lived in the part of the world later known as Syria struggled to create an independent civilization. Their geographical location was frequently prone to invasion because they were positioned between two immense and ancient kingdoms: Egypt and Sumeria. In the third and second millennia BC, the major powers of western Asia were the Egyptians, the Babylonians, and the Hittites. These were followed by the Assyrians, Chaldaeans (or Neo-Babylonians), and the Persians through the fourth century AD.

From the south and the north, Egypt and Sumeria spilled over into the borders that would later represent modern Syria. In 3200 BC, Egypt encompassed the coast as far as Byblos, an area that is now part of present-day Lebanon. Between 2677 and 2653 BC, the Sumerian warlord Lugalzaggisi raided the Syrian

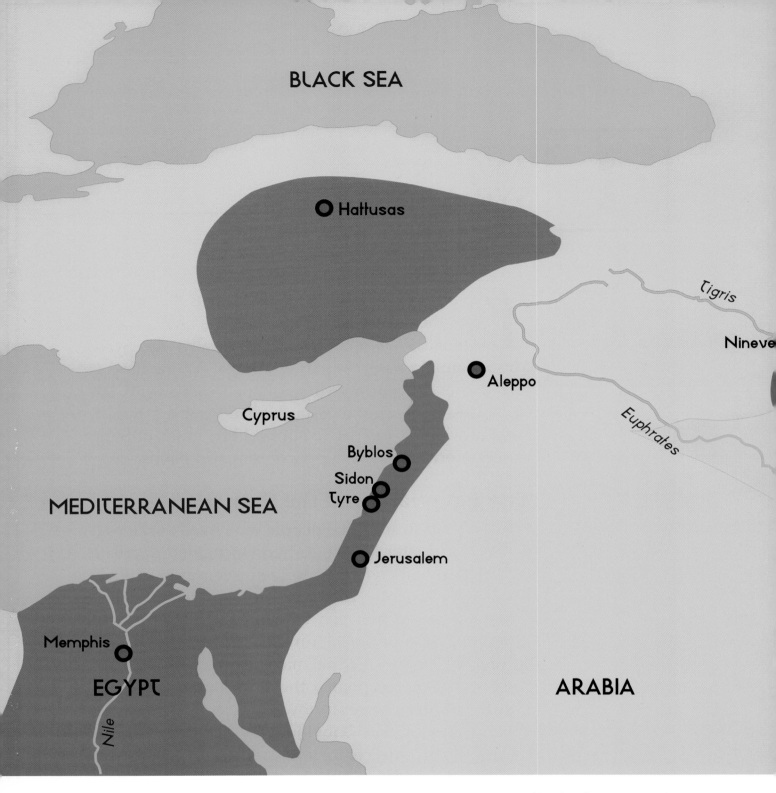

BLACK SEA

Tigris

Nineve

O Hattusas

Aleppo

Euphrates

Cyprus

Byblos

Sidon

Tyre

MEDITERRANEAN SEA

Jerusalem

Memphis

EGYPT

ARABIA

Nile

Trading routes in the Gulf region flourished in 1400 BC. Goods from territories inhabited by the Phoenicians and Assyrians headed south into Egypt and then across the Mediterranean Sea to coastal ports in Minoan and Mycenaean cities and the island of Crete. Caravan routes carrying precious metals, timber, and textiles were also valuable to cities and settlements throughout Mesopotamia. The Sumerian bull's head (top right) was once a part of an ancient stringed instrument. Now a part of the collection of Mesopotamian artifacts in the Pennsylvania University Museum in Philadelphia, it was originally found in a king's tomb in the Babylonian city of Ur.

A group of north Arabian nomads called the Amorites settled into the mountains that now mark the present-day Lebanese-Syrian border. The Amorites created bronze and used it to harden their weapons. In time, the Amorites' land became the southeastern border of Sumeria, and the Amorites became Sumerians. They founded the last Sumerian dynasty. Hammurabi, often remembered for his ancient law codes, was their last and greatest emperor. After his death, the Sumerian Empire collapsed.

The Phoenicians

After the Amorites, the Phoenicians dominated the Syrian region. The Greeks named the area "Phoenicia" because of a rare purple dye found only on the Syrian coast. The dye was made from a small mollusk. Only the most wealthy people could wear purple robes. Until the fall of the Byzantine Empire, purple robes remained a sign of importance.

The Phoenicians were great artisans. They forged weapons and tools of bronze, wove cloth, and used wheels to make pottery. The Phoenicians also carved ivory with great delicacy and made jewelry of silver and gold.

Phoenician engineering led to improved boatbuilding and navigation. The cedar trees of Lebanon, in

Babylon

BABYLONIA

Ur

Trade Empires

Hittite Empire c. 1400 BC

Assyrian Empire c. 1400 BC

Egyptian Empire c. 1400 BC

interior from its northern border to the Mediterranean coast.

These invasions brought weapons, goods, and settlers into ancient Syria.

This terra-cotta statue was among artifacts found in an ancient Mesopotamian site in Girsu, Iraq. Believed to be a shepherd carrying a lamb, experts have dated it to about 2000 BC.

distant countries. They carried the gold, incense, perfume, and spices of Arabia to Spain, where they collected valuable metals.

Along with goods, the Phoenicians carried ideas. They taught the traditions of one country to the people of another. The Phoenicians told of the achievements of Egypt and Mesopotamia. They also taught the Greeks how to navigate the ocean.

One of the greatest contributions of the Syria-based Phoenicians is the alphabet, which began as hieroglyphics. The Phoenicians created a phonetic alphabet. Their letters represented sounds. Just a few

the western region, made excellent ships. Known as the great sailors of the ancient world, the Phoenicians carried their goods all over the civilized world.

The earliest known sea routes of the Phoenicians followed the Mediterranean coast south to Egypt and north to the Aegean. In time, the Phoenicians learned to navigate the open sea by reading the stars. Eventually, they sailed through the Strait of Gibraltar into the Atlantic Ocean.

As an advanced seagoing people, the Phoenicians dominated trade in timber, wheat, olives, oil, wine, glass, ceramics, metalwork, horses, and slaves. Their sea routes linked

This artifact from the National Museum in Damascus dates from the Middle Syrian Period (1300 BC). A terra-cotta tablet with the imprinted seal of King Mursil II (1345–1320 BC), it was found in the archives of the ancient palace at Urgarit in Syria.

letters allowed people to spell every word in a language.

Before 1500 BC, the Phoenicians had developed an alphabet of twenty-two consonants. By 750 BC, the Greeks had added vowels to the Phoenician alphabet. The Romans then received this alphabet from the Greeks.

Another Syrian people who used the Phoenician alphabet were the Aramaeans. They adapted the alphabet to the needs of their language, Aramaic. From them, it passed to the Arabs, Indians, and Armenians.

The Aramaeans were originally Arabian nomads who entered Syria from the east. They were great land traders. In the ninth and eighth centuries BC, Aramaean control of the Syrian land trade matched Phoenician control of the seas.

Aramaean success in trade meant that the Aramaic language spread fast. By 500 BC, Aramaic was the major language of the Fertile Crescent. In time, the language divided. Syriac became the language of the churches of Syria, Lebanon, Palestine, and Mesopotamia. For one thousand years, it was the primary tongue of the Syrian people. It was displaced by Arabic in the thirteenth century.

The Hebrews

In the eighteenth century BC, a Semitic people called the Hebrews entered

Phoenician King Hazael of Damascus is the subject of this ivory carving found in an archaeological site in Syria. Dating from about 1000 BC, it is now housed in the Louvre Museum in Paris, France.

Syria. Five hundred years later, there was a great migration of Hebrews from Egypt. This is known as the Exodus. These people arrived in southwestern Syria looking for land. The Syrians lived in settled communities, traded for goods, and used written language. The Hebrews settled peacefully among them and farmed, built houses, and became literate.

At this time, an Indo-European people seized the south Syrian coast. They gave the region its later name of Palestine. The Philistines were warlike and knew how to forge iron. They wielded better weapons and wore stronger armor than the Hebrews did.

The Philistines tried to conquer the area, but the Hebrews refused to submit. They did not want to join a people with such different religious beliefs. The Hebrews were monotheists and believed in one God. The pantheistic Philistines believed in many divine spirits. The Hebrews rose against the Philistines under a Hebrew king.

The Philistines defeated the first Hebrew monarch, Saul, who came to power in 1020 BC. Saul's successor, David (1004–963 BC), drove out the Philistines and made Jerusalem his capital. After the reign of David's son Solomon (963–923 BC), the Hebrews split into two kingdoms: Israel and Judah.

In 721 BC, the Assyrian emperor Sargon II conquered Damascus and then Israel. Chaldaean, Syrian, and Arabian tribes joined the Assyrians. They largely pushed the Hebrews out of Syria. The Assyrians, Egyptians, and Chaldaeans fought among themselves. By 572, the Chaldaeans held the entire Syrian region.

The remaining Hebrews became citizens of Chaldea, along with the rest of the Syrians. This was a smooth shift. The Hebrews had adopted the Syrians' language and alphabet. They had learned their farming methods and developed artistically.

The Hebrews did leave one very important mark on Syrian culture: their religion. Hebrew monotheism of that time is recorded in the Old Testament of the Bible. In part, the Old Testament is a history of Hebrew prophets, the Exodus from Egypt, and the struggles with the Philistines. It describes ethics, codes of behavior, and the trials and rewards of faith.

The writings known as the Old Testament were a new kind of exploration of life and God. After the fall of the Hebrew nation, Hebrew ideas continued. The faithful maintained Hebrew culture. Modern believers still find the ancient writings relevant. Like the invention of the alphabet, these texts are a great Syrian gift to human culture.

The Chaldaeans lost Syria to the Persians in 538 BC. Syria and Palestine dissolved into a Persian Empire that stretched from Egypt to Asia Minor to India. This empire had standardized currency and roads, and a single language: Aramaic. Syria was part of a province that included Palestine and Cyprus. Damascus was the capital. This lasted until the middle of the fourth century.

2 | SYRIA AND ROME

Syria's rise ended when Alexander the Great conquered Persia (Iran) between 334 and 330 BC. Alexander's victory spread the Greek culture of Hellenism east to India, where it held sway for 200 years. After Alexander's death in 323 BC, his generals divided his empire. Seleucus took Syria and Palestine, and Syria became part of the Seleucid dynasty.

Syrian Christianity

Syrian culture of the Philistines and Semites was different from Greek and, later, Roman culture. Syrian Jews and Zoroastrians fought the invasion of Greek pantheism (the worship of many gods) by spreading their own monotheistic ideas.

Syria's Christian writings, including the Gospels, are among the most important texts in history. Originally written in Aramaic, the works describe the teachings of Jesus of Nazareth. Jesus was born the son of a Jewish carpenter. He became a religious teacher. His followers, Christians, believed he was the son of God. During the reign of the Roman emperor Tiberius, Jesus was sentenced to death by crucifixion.

According to his believers, Jesus was born of a virgin mother, Mary. While he lived, he performed miracles. After his death, he returned from the dead and rose to heaven.

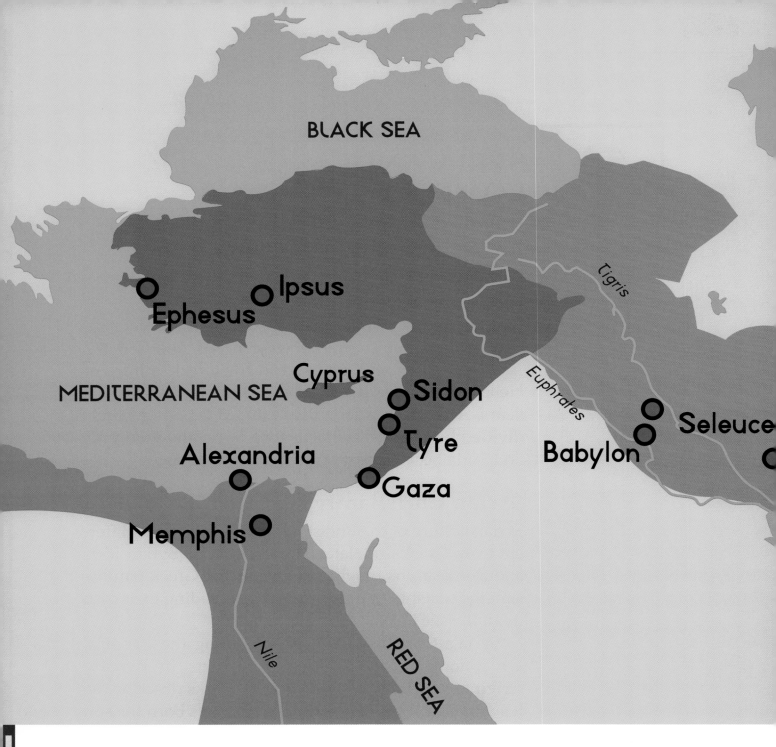

BLACK SEA

Tigris

Ipsus

Ephesus

Euphrates

Cyprus

MEDITERRANEAN SEA

Sidon

Seleuce

Tyre

Babylon

Alexandria

Gaza

Memphis

Nile

RED SEA

By 275 BC, or about forty-eight years after the death of Alexander the Great, three Hellenistic kingdoms had emerged from the descending leadership of the original generals who had fought for his Asian empire in the War of the Diadochi (Successors). Although Antigonus, Seleucus, and Ptolemy were strong enough to lead the kingdoms in Alexander's place, they could not keep out the Romans, who captured Macedonia in 148 BC, Syria in 64 BC, and Egypt in 30 BC.

CASPIAN
SEA

Alexandria Eskhata
(Kokand)

Alexandria Areia
(Herat)

a
Susa

Persepolis

PERSIAN GULF

Pura

Three Hellenistic Kingdoms, c. 275 BC

Kingdom under Ptolemy

Kingdom under Antigonus

Kingdom under Seleucus

Arabian Sea

Christianity reached out to all people. Jesus offered hope to people who were poor, had been cast out of society, or had sinned and were willing to repent. To be a good Christian believer, a person did not need money, social status, or scholarly knowledge. A person needed only to have faith in Jesus and to act in a moral way.

Christianity attracted passionate followers. Monotheistic Jews converted to Christianity, as did the followers of traditional faiths. The Roman government watched the swift spread of this new religion, fearing it might interfere with their control over the region. To discourage it, they harassed Christian priests and followers.

Syria's early Christian priests worried the Romans might try to outlaw Christianity. In response, they Hellenized Christian practices and rituals. This made Christianity more acceptable. Soon, Greeks and Romans joined the swelling ranks of Christian converts. For three hundred years, the popularity of Christianity grew. Early in the fourth century, Emperor Constantine made it the official religion of the Roman Empire.

In AD 193, Syrian influence reached the Roman throne directly. Emperor Septimius Severus (193–211) was married to a Syrian woman named Julia Domna. Her father was a Christian priest from Homs (Emesa). When Septimius Severus died, their sons, Caracalla and Geta, became co-emperors. Julia Domna wielded power through them. In 212, Caracalla had Geta murdered. Five years later, he himself died. Forced to retire from public life, Julia Domna killed herself.

Julia Domna's younger sister, Julia Maesa, continued the Syrian dynasty. She took power for her two grandsons, Elagabalus and Alexander Severus. First she supported Elagabalus, who ruled from 218 to 222, and then Alexander, who held the throne from 222 to 235.

MEDITERRANEAN SEA

Alexandria

EGYPT

Nile

BLACK SEA

Antioch

SYRIA

CYPRUS

Damascus

ARABIA

This map of the Roman Empire, circa 200 BC–AD 106, shows Syrian territories under Roman leadership. It was during this time that Roman roads were built through Syria linking important legionary forts *(above)* of the Roman military. Pompey the Great *(top left)* was elected to the Roman consul in 70 BC after proving himself an able fighter and general for the Roman army. Along with Julius Caesar and Crassus, Pompey later ruled the empire in the First Triumvirate from 60 BC.

RED SEA

Alexander took power at the age of thirteen. His rule was more successful than those of his brother and Julia Domna's sons. He disliked lavish living and led a quieter life. He lowered taxes and supported science and art. His war against the Persians reclaimed Mesopotamia for Rome. He ruled until the age of twenty-six, when he was killed in a mutiny.

In 244, another Syrian took the Roman throne. He was known as Philip the Arab. In 248, Philip oversaw the celebration of Rome's one thousandth birthday. One year later, he was killed and the Syrian influence in Rome ended.

Despite their loss of imperial power, Syrians were growing stronger. During the second and third centuries, Syrians built trading centers along the Mediterranean and inland. Merchants took control of the trade of wines, spices, grain, glassware, fabrics, and jewelry.

Historians believe the rare fresco seen in this photograph was created about 244 BC as a part of a Syrian Christian house of worship known as Dura Europas. Archaeologists believe it was once a private residence and was converted to serve Syria's earliest Christian community. Now a part of the National Museum in Damascus, it depicts scenes from the Old Testament.

The Greco-Roman ruins pictured here were a part of the desert city of Palmyra, or the city of palm trees. Once an ancient stomping ground for passing caravans en route from the Persian Gulf to the Mediterranean and along the Silk Road, Palmyra was made wealthy by taxing passing merchants. A Roman vassal state from AD 129 under Emperor Hadrian, by 272 Palmyra had become a full Roman colony. Pictured here is the site of an ancient theater and the Temple of Bel, one of the three gods of the city. Today Palmyra, sometimes referred to as the "city of a thousand columns," is known as Tadmor. It remains one of Syria's premier tourist attractions.

The Sacking of Palmyra

One of the most important Roman trade centers was Palmyra. A gateway between Rome and Parthia (Iran), Palmyra had been a thriving natural oasis since at least 1100 BC. Water gushed from its springs and wells. According to Arab storytellers, a genie had conjured its enchanting architecture for King Solomon. To this day, its ruins are spectacular.

Palmyra formed a crucial trade link in east-west and north-south directions. When the Roman emperor Hadrian took power in AD 117, he realized the city was as important for war as it was for trade. Hadrian offered the Palmyrenes a deal: He made the city a vassal (subordinate) of Rome, which gave Palmyra certain trading privileges but did not interfere with its government. This secured Palmyra's loyalty. When the Sassanids, who had replaced the Parthians, waged war on Rome, the Palmyrenes sided with the Romans.

In AD 260, the Sassanid Shapur I captured the Roman emperor Valerian. Also, he conquered a large part of Syria. The chieftain of Palmyra, Odenathus, saw that the time had come for Palmyra to prove its loyalty to Rome. His armies routed Shapur from Syria and forced him back to the gates of his capital at Ctesiphon.

Delighted with Odenathus's success, the Romans made him Roman vice-emperor of the eastern Roman Empire, which included Syria, part of Asia Minor, and northern Arabia. Unfortunately, his title was short-lived. In AD 266, Odenathus and his oldest son were assassinated at Homs

EASTERN HALF
OF THE
ROMAN EMPIRE

English Miles

BALTIC SEA

SARMATIA

SCYTHIA

Danube R.
Vindobona (Vienna)
ICUM
PANNONIA
Carnuntum
Bregetio
Siscia
Mursa
Cibalae
SIRMIUM
Singidunum (Belgrade)
Viminacium
The Iron Gates
Trajan's Bridge
Abricium
Naissus
Margus
MŒSIA
Nicopolis
Sistova
Sardica
Marcianople
Varna
Mardia
Succi Pass
Philippopolis
Hadrianople
MACEDONIA
THRACE
Heraclea
Philippi
Nicopolis
CONSTANTINOPLE
Bosphorus
Berea
Thessalonica
NICOMEDIA
Chalcedon
Nicaea
Thessaly
Sea of Marmora
Actium
Cyzicus
Apollonia
Prusa
Dadastana
BITHYNIA
Delphi
Troas
MYSIA
Ancyra
Athens
Pergamum
Thyatira
Sardis
PONTUS
MINOR
Corinth
Smyrna
Philadelphia
Phrygia
Galatia
Sparta
Ephesus
Laodicea
ASIA
Iconium
Cappadocia
Patmos
Miletus
Lystra
Derbe
Isauria
Tyana
Lycia
CILICIA
Mopsuestia
Crete
Rhodes
Phœnix
Tarsus
Issus

DACIA
Sarmizegethusa

Theiss R.
Dniester R.
Dnieper R.

Ad Salices
Crimea
Cherson
Mæotis
Lazica
Colchis
Caucasus Mts.
Iberia
Albania
Gangara

BLACK SEA

Phasis
Trapezus
Mt. Ararat
ARMENIA
Araxes R.
Arzanene
Carduene
Urumiyah L.
Azerbiyan
Van L.
Salban
Martyropolis
Thebarmes
Ganzaca
Sebastoplis
Halys R.
Caesarea
Amida
Dara
Niabis
Bezabde
Media
Edessa
Singara
Nineveh
Carrhae
Hierapolis
Callicinum
Resaina
Hatra
Assyria
ANTIOCH
Berœa
Euphrates R.
Mesopotamia
Tigris R.
Dura
PERSIAN
Circesium
Anatha
Perisabor
Arba R.
Bumera
Ecbatana
Salamis
Emesa
Palmyra
Kufa (Bagdad)
CTESIPHON
EMPIRE
Aspadana (Ispahan)
Heliopolis
Ruins of Babylon
Babylonia
Susa
Baalbek
Damascus
Susiana
Tyre
Kerbela
Caesarea
Palestine
Yarmuk R.
Arabian
Joppa
Jerusalem
Orchoe (Ur of the Chaldees)
Teredon
Bethlehem
Desert
ALEXANDRIA
Pelusium
PERSIAN GULF
Cyrene
Bilbeis
Danin
Heliopolis
Ajnadein
Petra
Memphis
Babylon
Arsinoe
ARABIA
Ælana

MEDITERRANEAN SEA

Cyprus

Libyan Desert
EGYPT

Ibium
Antinoe

Arabicus
Sinus

N.B. The Succi Pass does not cross the Balkan Mountains, but crosses a spur from the Balkan Mountains which runs towards the south-west.

ILLYRICUM
DALMATIA
ADRIATIC SEA
EPIRUS

Longitude East of Greenwich

Lithographed by W.& A.K.Johnston, Limited, Edinburgh & London.

Under the leadership of Constantine, the eastern and western halves of the Roman Empire were officially united under Christianity in 324. However, the Roman Empire had divided again by 395, and this historic map shows the eastern portion after that division. By 476, the western portion had crumbled under invasions by the Visigoths, but the eastern half, known as Byzantium, continued until 1453. This map was originally printed in *East and West Through Fifteen Centuries, Vol II,* by G. F. Young, which was published in 1916.

(Emesa); it is believed that the Romans arranged for these murders.

Outraged by the murder of her husband and son, Odenathus's wife, Zenobia, took power, declaring herself Queen of the East. Her first act, in defiance of Rome, was to increase her power and territory. Two excellent generals, Zabbay and Zabda, spearheaded her ambitious campaigns. Zenobia swiftly seized Egypt from Rome, named her young son its king, and issued new Egyptian coins without Roman symbols. She conquered much of Asia Minor and forced the Roman garrisons back to Ankara, in present-day Turkey.

Under Emperor Aurelian, the Romans rallied. They first fought Zenobia at Antioch and later at Homs. Here, they defeated Zabda. Finally, in AD 272, the Romans captured Palmyra. Zenobia escaped into the desert, but the Romans hunted her down and dragged her to Rome in chains. Later, the Romans supported her there until her death.

Back in Palmyra, the Palmyrenes overwhelmed the Roman troops and reclaimed their city. Furious at this rebellion, Aurelian returned and burned Palmyra to the ground. He destroyed its walls, shut down its government, and looted its magnificent Temple of the Sun. In Rome, Aurelian filled a new temple with Palmyra's fabulous ornaments and statues. The new temple stood as a testament to Rome's victory. For Syria, it was a bitter reminder of the harshness of the Hellenic invaders.

From Rome to Byzantium

For a period, the Romans maintained their military power in the eastern empire, but the anger of the Palmyrenes was a sign of things to come. Meanwhile, the spread of Syrian culture continued. Syrian Christians built churches near trading centers. This maintained the distinctly Syrian flavor of Christianity and introduced the Christian cross into Europe.

As the Syrians continued to expand their influence, the Roman Empire stumbled. It had overtaxed the peoples of its various provinces. Many of these regions had local cultures that were not Roman. They did not want to pay taxes to a distant Roman government that did not understand their interests.

Rome was also under attack by other foreign powers. This divided its attention and weakened its hold on Syria. Even worse, traditional Roman ideas were crumbling. To survive, Rome needed to transform itself into a cultural power that could accept and use the new ideas of Christianity. This new power would become the Byzantine Empire.

3 | THE RISE OF ISLAM

Mecca lies in the southwest of the Arabian Peninsula, in what is now Saudi Arabia. It was originally a polytheistic shrine. Polytheists are worshipers who believe in more than one god. The polytheists of Arabia worshiped their gods through idols, which were small statues of wood and rock. Many Arab nomads visited the Ka'aba in Mecca to worship the great Black Stone, which is a meteorite. The Black Stone is believed to have been put in the Ka'aba by Abraham, who is considered a prophet of Islam.

The Prophet Muhammad

In the fifth century AD, Mecca was the trade capital of the Arabian Peninsula and is now a holy city for Muslims. The prophet Muhammad, Islam's founder, was born there in AD 571.

This historic map of Egypt, Palestine, and Arabia was conceived by the famous seventeenth-century Dutch cartographer Willem Janszoon Blaeu (1571–1638), who was also responsible for publishing later editions of *Theatrum Orbis Terrarum* (also known as the Atlas Novus, or the New Atlas) after the death of Abraham Ortelius. Among the most renowned mapmakers of his day, Blaeu later became the official cartographer for the British East India Company.

MARE MEDITERRANEUM

MARE

TERRA SANCTA
quae in Sacris
Terra Promissionis olim
PALESTINA

Amstelodami
Ex officina Guilielmi Blaeuw 1629

Muslims believe that Muhammad was the last prophet in a line that includes Abraham, Moses, and Jesus.

Muhammad spent his early life as a merchant, doing business with both Jews and Christians. He admired their spirituality and morality. However, most Jews and Christians disdained Arabs as infidels, or unbelievers. Muhammad knew his people were too proud to join a religion whose followers despised them.

By the time he was forty years of age, Muhammad's spirituality grew deeper. He retreated into the hills outside Mecca to pray and meditate. One night, according to Muslim beliefs, the archangel Gabriel appeared to Muhammad and revealed the word of Allah, or God. In AD 613, Muhammad began to preach that there was only one God, that people must not worship idols, that the virtuous would go to paradise and the wicked to damnation,

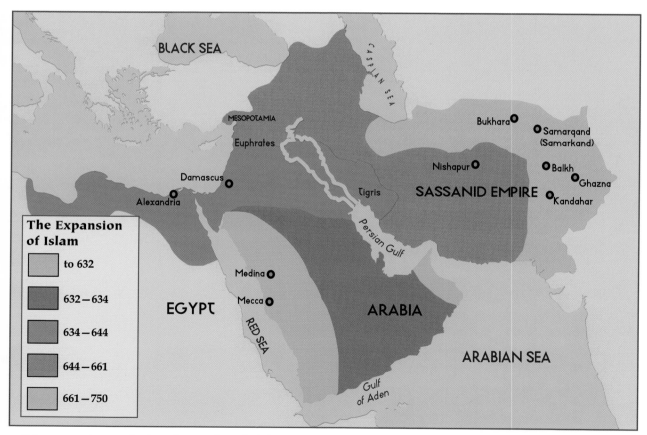

The Expansion of Islam

- to 632
- 632–634
- 634–644
- 644–661
- 661–750

Prior to AD 610, Arabs largely worshiped idols at the shrine of the Ka'aba, the center of the Great Mosque in the city of Mecca. Even the Islamic book of revelations, the Koran, was not written until approximately 644—more than a decade after the death of Muhammad. By 629, Muslims had entered Mecca, from where Muhammad had been previously cast out, and since that time the city has become the center of Muslim prayer, replacing Jerusalem. Islam had followers throughout the Middle East by 750, as shown in this map.

and that he himself was the messenger of God.

Muhammad's early sermons were short passages of rhythmic prose. According to Islamic beliefs, Allah dictated the words that Muhammad recited. Muhammad's disciples copied the verses onto leather, palm leaves, or camel bone. Eventually, they grouped them into chapters called *surahs*.

These surahs make up the Koran, the Islamic holy book. "Koran" means "recitation" in Arabic.

Muhammad taught people to forsake idols and nature spirits and instead worship Allah, the one true God. The word "Muslim" (practitioner of the faith of Islam) means "one who submits his will to God." The word "Islam" means "total submission."

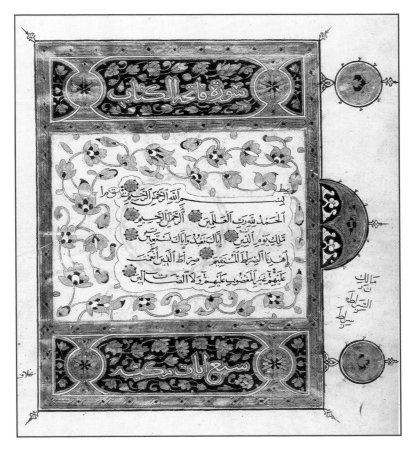

The manuscript page shown here is part of an ornamentally decorated Koran that dates from 1389. It is now housed in the Bayrische Staatsbibliothek in Munich, Germany.

The Spread of Islam

Because Mecca was a profitable trading center, its merchants did not like the idea of removing its idols. Meccans making money by charging the Arab nomads who visited and worshiped the meteorite known as the Black Stone worried that Muhammad's ideas would discourage their business. The Meccans' irritation at Muhammad's insistence quickly grew into anger. Soon, threats and attacks made Mecca dangerous. Even though some Meccans discouraged the spread of Islam, others, especially those among the lower classes, embraced the social justice aspect of Islam. Soon, Muhammad left Mecca for the city of Yathrib, 300 miles (483 kilometers) to the northeast.

Several rival tribes controlled Yathrib. Their leaders needed someone to settle tribal disputes. As Muhammad was above tribal loyalties, the Yathribites welcomed his guidance. Muhammad became the *imam*, or leader, of Yathrib. He taught people to obey Allah and practice Arab honor and loyalty. The year 622, in which Muhammad moved to Yathrib, is the start of the Muslim calendar. Yathrib is now Medinat al-Nabi ("City of the Prophet"), or Medina.

Muhammad was a political and religious leader. He led Medina to a military victory over Mecca. In 630, he turned the Ka'aba into a Muslim sanctuary. After the battle, he treated the defeated Meccans with respect. Afterward, most converted to Islam.

Islam Unites the Arabs

As Muhammad spread the word of Allah, he united the Arabian Peninsula. More and more tiny Arab tribes answered to Muhammad and to Islam. Starting with the first revelation, Muhammad began to make new laws. In a culture that preferred sons to daughters so much that female infants were often killed or abandoned, he forbade the killing of baby girls. He allowed women to own and inherit property, limited the number of wives a man could have to four, and outlawed people with vendettas from taking more than they had lost, in money or in blood.

Muhammad also created a code of behavior. Muslims do not drink alcohol, gamble, or eat pork or blood. Every Muslim must pray, fast, give alms or charity, and, if able, make the pilgrimage to Mecca, the holy site and the birthplace of Muhammad. These four "acts of devotion," plus the profession of faith ("there is but one God and Muhammad is his apostle"), are the Five Pillars of Islam.

For Muslims, Islam is the final stage of monotheism. It expresses the true vision of God, unlike Judaism and Christianity, which, in their opinion, went astray. In the eyes of Muslims, Islam is the perfect revelation of Allah's word. It is also perfect in its simplicity and direct relationship with Allah. Islam has no priests, rabbis, bishops, or popes. The *imam* leads the prayer but does not tell believers how to behave. Every devout Muslim is equal in the eyes of Allah.

4 WARS OF FAITH

Muhammad died in AD 632. His successor was Abu Bakr, the *kalifat rasul-Allah*, or "successor to the apostle of Allah." "Kalifat" is the origin of the Arab title of *caliph*. A caliph is the civil and religious leader of a kingdom called a caliphate. Abu Bakr was Muhammad's father-in-law and the first of the four rightly guarded (orthodox) caliphs. Abu Bakr wanted to create an immense Arab Muslim state. He gathered the Arabian tribes into a nation and looked abroad to expand his borders.

Islam Enters Syria

At that time, Persia and Roman Byzantium were the two great powers in the Middle East, though each was struggling. Byzantium's major provinces were Syria and Egypt, and its rule was unpopular in both places. In Syria, the trouble was one of religion. The Syrians were non-Hellenic Christians who were persecuted under the Byzantines as heretics. For Abu Bakr, a Muslim, this unpopularity was an opportunity. Because Syria had no real loyalty to the Byzantine Empire, it could easily join the Arab caliphate.

The sudden attack by Abu Bakr's fierce Arab army shocked Byzantium. The highly trained Byzantines were totally unprepared for the onslaught they encountered while riding into Syria. In 634, they fought and lost a battle at Ajnadayn in southern Palestine. After Abu Bakr's death, his successor, Omar, continued the Arab advance. Omar took Damascus in 636 and Jerusalem in 638, driving Hellenism forever from the East.

The decay of the Byzantine Empire and the disgruntlement of local Syrians only partly explain the Arabs' astonishing military victories. Abu Bakr's tribal warriors had, by Roman standards, little training. They used none of the complex formation tactics, then common in traditional warfare, and had no siege equipment.

The Arabs' battle strategy was to ride in a line, mounted on horses and camels, within a spear's throw of the enemy. From there, they pelted the Roman soldiers with javelins. Then they retreated,

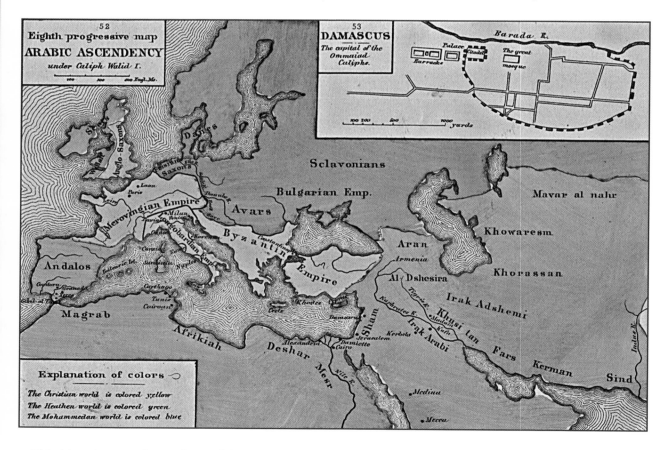

This historic map shows the Arabic Empire at its greatest extent beginning in the eighth century. Taken from *A Historical Atlas Containing a Chronological Series of One Hundred and Four Maps, at Successive Periods, From the Dawn of History to the Present Day*, it was written by Robert H. Labberton and dates from 1884. Damascus, then the Arab capital under the Umayyad dynasty, is shown as an inset on the top right.

rearmed, and charged again. When the enemy line broke, they galloped into the crush and fought using hand-to-hand combat.

In 639, the Arab general Muawiya became governor of Syria. Generals such as Muawiya are credited with the Arabs' smooth sweep into Syria, Persia, and Europe. A member of the Umayyad family (as was Muhammad's widow, Aisha), Muawiya was a superb strategist. In Syria, despite his desert roots, he created a navy that challenged the ancient sea power of Byzantium.

Muawiya's political philosophy was to use force as a last resort. He was known to have said, "I apply not my lash where my tongue suffices, nor my sword where my whip is enough. If there be one hair binding me to my fellow men, I'll let it not break. If they pull, I loosen; if they loosen, I pull."

The Sunnis and the Shiites

Syria was clearly more important geographically than the Arabian wastelands around Mecca and Medina. When the Arabs recognized this, Muawiya's power increased. He decided to rise against the caliph. The caliph at that time was Ali, Muhammad's cousin and son-in-law.

Ali took power after the murder of Uthman, the successor of Omar.

His wife, Fatima, had been Muhammad's favorite daughter. Ali was popular, devout, and courageous, though he did have enemies. Aisha, the prophet's widow, loathed him. In December 656, she and his rivals rode against him in the Battle of the Camel, named for the camel Aisha rode into the fight. When Ali triumphed, he finally felt secure on his throne. He moved his capital to Mesopotamia, in present-day Iraq, and settled down to rule the Arab Empire, though he did not anticipate Muawiya's wrath.

Muawiya declared himself Uthman's avenger. In Damascus, he displayed not only Uthman's bloodied shirt but also the severed fingers of Uthman's wife, Nailah, lost while trying to defend him. Muawiya insisted Ali either find the murderers or admit his guilt. If Ali stepped down, Syria would be the capital and center of the Arab world, not Mesopotamia.

Muawiya's soldiers met Ali's at Siffin, on the western bank of the Euphrates River, near the Syria-Mesopotamia border. The battle dragged on for several weeks. In July 657, Ali's forces were close to victory. At this point, Muawiya's war leader, General Amr ibn al-As, devised a plan. Amr's men tied copies of the Koran to their spears

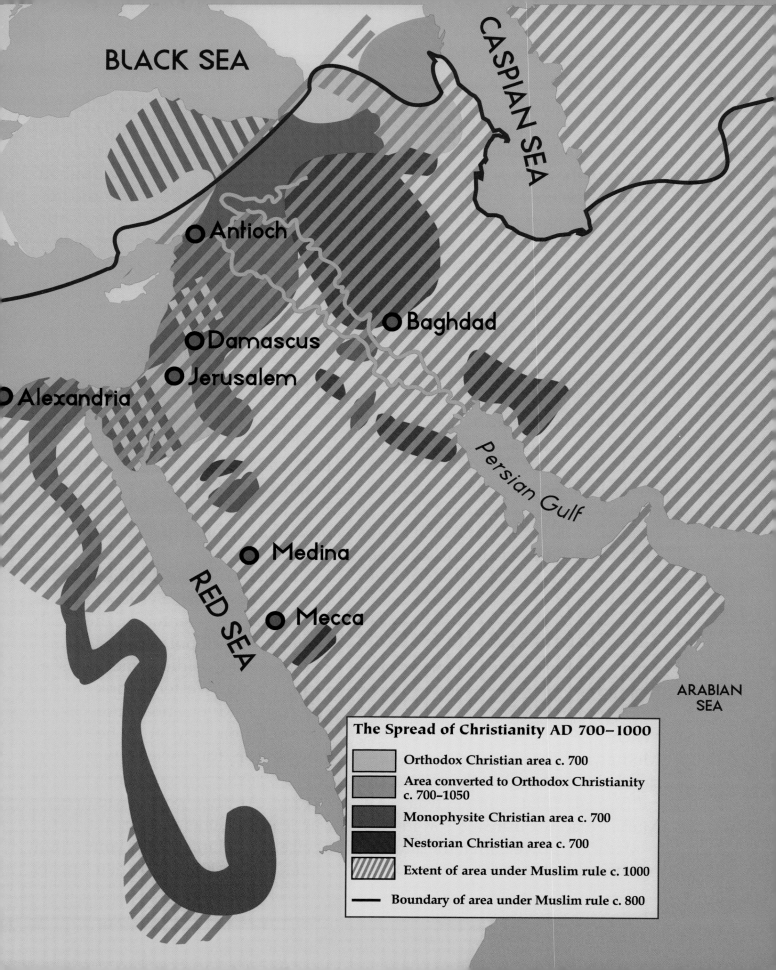

BLACK SEA

CASPIAN SEA

O Antioch

O Baghdad

O Damascus

O Jerusalem

O Alexandria

Persian Gulf

O Medina

O Mecca

RED SEA

ARABIAN SEA

The Spread of Christianity AD 700–1000

Orthodox Christian area c. 700

Area converted to Orthodox Christianity c. 700–1050

Monophysite Christian area c. 700

Nestorian Christian area c. 700

Extent of area under Muslim rule c. 1000

Boundary of area under Muslim rule c. 800

and raised them to heaven. Ali's soldiers hesitated. Muawiya suggested they discuss terms rather than spill Muslim blood.

No record remains of the meeting, but the decision to halt was a mistake for Ali. Before, he was a nearly victorious caliph. Afterward, he was arguing for his own throne with a common governor. Disgusted with this turn of events, a large group of Ali's men deserted him. They declared that only Allah could decide such an outcome. These men became Kharijites, or seceders. Four years later, in January 661, a Kharijite struck Ali on the forehead with a poisoned saber and killed him.

Once dead, Ali became a powerful symbol, far more influential than he had been while alive. His supporters called themselves the Shi'a, or partisans, of Ali. They believed only Ali and his descendants had the right to rule the caliphate. The Umayyads, led by Muawiya, insisted Muhammad's successor should be elected, according to the tradition, or *sunna*, of the desert. Muawiya and his followers became known as Sunnis.

Today, the rift between the Sunnis and the Shiites still divides Islam. Ninety percent of the world's Muslims are Sunnis, but the Shiite population is significant in Syria, Lebanon, Iraq, Yemen, and eastern Arabia. Since the sixteenth century, Shiism has been the ruling faith in Iran.

The Umayyads and the 'Abbasids

The victorious Muawiya joined Syria and Egypt into a single territory and became caliph in Jerusalem. Muawiya is generally considered the architect of the Islamic Empire, and Syria under his rule became the most prosperous province of the caliphate. Ali's eldest son, Hassan, tried and failed to fight Muawiya from Mesopotamia. Despite the democratic sunna, or tradition of the desert, Muawiya left his throne to his son Yazid. After Muawiya's death in 680, Ali's younger son, Hussein, died in another doomed revolt against the Umayyads. This is an important event in Shi'a Islam and is known as the Battle of Karbala. After Hussein declared

Although Christian minority groups existed in parts of Egypt and Arabia, Christianity largely flourished in Europe, where the Western (Latin) and Eastern (Greek Orthodox) traditions gained their greatest converts. During the period of 1095-1291, the Crusades to the Holy Land (Palestine) by Europeans attempted to recapture what they believed were Christian lands from the Muslims. Conversion to Christianity was especially great during and after the fourteenth century, when European plagues known as the Black Death contributed to millions of human losses between 1347 and 1352.

himself the legitimate caliph, he decided to travel from Mecca to Kufah. The governor of the region posted patrols along his route, and Hussein was asked to surrender at Karbala. When he refused, he was killed along with his 200 men. The day of his death became a day of mourning for the Shiites, who consider his tomb in Karbala the holiest place in the world. To a Shiite Muslim, a pilgrimage to Karbala is a more devout act than one to Mecca.

The Umayyads were the first Islamic dynasty. Under it, the Arab Empire expanded. By 717, the Arabs held Sicily, Portugal, and most of Spain, and had crossed the Pyrenees into France. In 732, the eastern border of the Arab Empire stretched to Punjab in present-day Pakistan and Samarkand in present-day Uzbekistan.

The Umayyads did not force Islam on their subjects. During early Umayyad rule, Syria remained largely

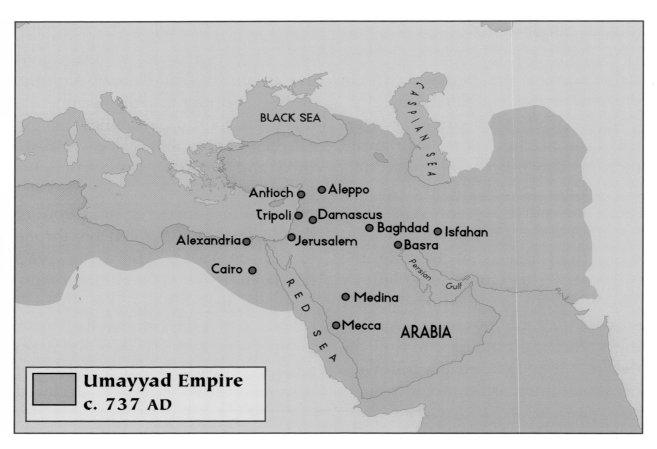

Umayyad Empire c. 737 AD

This illustration depicts the Arab territories of the Umayyad Empire at its height of power. The Umayyads ruled the empire for some eighty-nine years, accomplishing much for the Arab world, including expanding foreign trade relationships, gaining wealth, organizing the military, and making great improvements in the lives of most Muslims.

The Birth of Islamic Art

The artists of Umayyad Syria blended the styles of the Arabs, Persian, Syrians, and Greeks. This was the birth of Islamic art. The Arabs contributed patterns and repetition. The long rows of columns in mosques and palaces are like the rows of straight date palms at an oasis. The Greeks provided symmetry and the elegance of simplicity. From the Persians, the Umayyads borrowed delicacy and color. When the Umayyads fell to the 'Abbasids in 754, Syria ceased to be the center of the Islamic world. The 'Abbasids moved their capital to Kufah, in Iraq. During the Golden Age of Islam, Islamic art flourished. 'Abbasid rulers encouraged painting, poetry, and science throughout the Arab Empire. They built hospitals and improved medicine. Scholars translated Greek, Roman, and Indian texts into Arabic. Mathematicians developed algebra and invented the concept of zero. The period also witnessed the construction of the world's first observatory and the invention of the astrolabe.

Built during the eighth century, the Umayyad Mosque in Damascus with its treasury tower and courtyard—once considered the safest place for the Muslim community to store its valuables—is pictured in this contemporary photograph. The site on which the mosque stands has a long religious history. Once the site of a temple shrine to the Roman god Jupiter, later during Syria's Christian era the same site was home to a cathedral dedicated to John the Baptist.

Christian. However, the Umayyads did "Arabize" their territories. They changed the official language of their empire from Aramaic to Arabic. They minted the first purely Arab coins, created a postal service, and built Islam's third holiest sanctuary after Mecca and Medina—the Dome of the Rock—in Jerusalem. The regime also laid roads, dug canals, and irrigated new land for farming. The great Umayyad poets wrote *ghazals*, or love poems, and political works, which criticized politicians much like modern newspapers do.

During this era, Damascus, and therefore Syria, was the capital of the Arab Empire. Beyond the Syrian border, the anger of other Islamic groups simmered. The Iraqi Shiites viewed the Syrian Umayyads as unlawful usurpers. They did not approve of the Umayyad separation of government and religion. The Kharijite extremists, who had splintered from the Shiites, shared the Shiites' disdain for the Umayyads.

The Kharijites and the Shiites came together to form a revolutionary movement, led by the 'Abbasids, named for Muhammad's uncle, 'Abbas. Syria fell to the 'Abbasids at the Battle of the Zab in 750, though Damascus held out for another few months. On April 26, 750, after a siege of several days, the capital surrendered. One member of the royal family, Prince Abdul Rahman, escaped and fled to Spain. Once there, he started a new Umayyad dynasty that ruled Moorish (Arab) Spain for 300 years.

The fall of the Umayyads meant the end of Syria's glory as the center of the Arab Empire. The 'Abbasids moved their capital from Damascus to Baghdad, near the older capital of Ctesiphon.

The 'Abbasids killed most of the remaining Umayyads. 'Abbas himself took on the name al-Saffah, or "blood shedder." His propagandist declared that the destruction of the 'Abbasid caliphate would throw the entire universe into chaos. They effaced the names of Umayyad rulers from buildings and destroyed the tombs of every Umayyad caliph except Muawiya and Umar II.

Although the 'Abbasids were more culturally sophisticated than the Umayyads, they were less tolerant. Many Syrians were forced to convert to Islam. Others converted to avoid heavy taxes. The Umayyads had maintained the custom of the desert sheikh, who generally governs by listening to his people. The 'Abbasids believed their kings were not merely human rulers but the shadows of Allah on Earth.

5 THE EUROPEAN CRUSADES AGAINST ISLAM

In 1095, Pope Urban II declared the Muslims to be usurpers of the Holy Land. He urged Christians to wage war upon them insisting that it was the will of God. By the spring of 1097, roughly 150,000 men, mostly French, had set out on foot for Constantinople. Officially, the Crusades were a holy war on the religion of Islam. Much of Europe's interest in the Middle East, however, was economic. There was not enough money in Europe. Men with no inheritance were often forced to choose between the priesthood and the army. For many, the Crusades meant adventure and treasure.

Over the span of nearly 200 years, Europe launched eight Crusades against the East. The primary target was Jerusalem in the Holy Land of Palestine, birthplace of Jesus Christ. Much of the conflict focused on Syria's Mediterranean coast. The Syrian ports offered direct sea access from Europe's wealthy merchant cities to the riches of India and China.

The Early Crusades

At the time of the First Crusade, Syria's rulers were Seljuk Turks. The Seljuks had traveled from central Asia, toppled the 'Abbasids, and seized the northern Arab Empire. They were Sunni Muslims. The Egyptian Fatimids held the south. They were Shiites.

Oz, estoit aguant merueille la cite de
sur, et moit enciennie. Vlpin qui moit
fuit cedois istuties, sicom tend it. Hi ou me in
jennorerent mout quiant ilozent la seigno
rie del mon de selonc le tenciennies estoire. ba

This manuscript page depicting the siege of Antioch by Christians in 1098 during the First Crusade was part of a historical work entitled the *History of Deeds Done Beyond the Sea* by William of Tyre (1130–1185), a Christian historian. Antioch, an ancient city founded in 300 BC by Seleucus and named for his father, Antiochus, later became a Roman stronghold and a city where Jesus's followers were first known as Christians.

As these ruling factions fought for control over it, the division split and weakened the Arab Empire.

The Seljuks were also busy fighting a violent sect called the Assassins or "hashish-eaters," a group that specialized in political murders. The Assassins manufactured poisoned knives, sent messages by carrier pigeon, and never questioned an order. A high-level Assassin once proved this obedience by ordering two men to leap to their deaths from a castle tower.

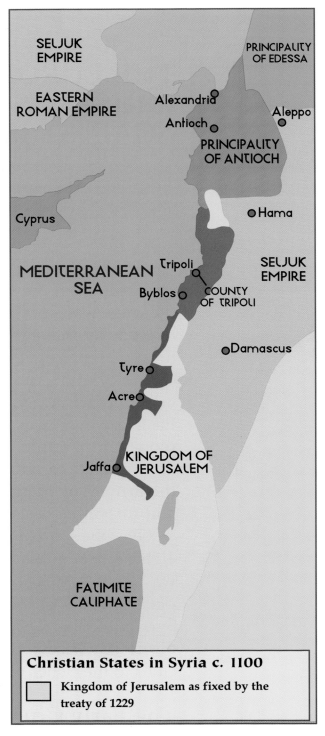

Christian States in Syria c. 1100

Kingdom of Jerusalem as fixed by the treaty of 1229

Four Christian states, including Jerusalem, Tripoli (in present-day Lebanon), Antioch (in present-day Syria), and Edessa (in present-day Turkey) existed in the Middle East around 1100. All were subject to leadership under the pope and each relied upon a feudalistic structure for land ownership.

The Seljuks' conflicts distracted them from the approach of the crusaders. In July 1099, the Christians took Jerusalem. From there, they moved up the Syrian coast. After an eight-year siege, in 1107, the crucial port town of Tripoli fell to the crusaders. Beirut and Sidon followed in 1110. Aleppo, Hama, Homs, and Damascus remained in Arab hands but were forced to pay taxes.

Finally, under Imad-al-Din Zangi, the Muslims began to rally. In 1144, Zangi seized the city of Edessa and drove the crusaders from the area between Syria and Iraq. This victory marked the beginning of a new period of Muslim successes. It also provoked the Second Crusade, which lasted from 1147 to 1149, laid siege to Damascus for only four days, and accomplished nothing.

Saladin

Born into an established Kurdish family, Saladin (1137–1193) was concerned more with religion and scholarship than warfare as a young man, though he later matured into a ruler with a firm hand. In 1169, at the age of thirty-one, he was appointed military general as well as *vizier*, or executive officer, of Syrian troops in Egypt. As his talents for leadership became more obvious, he rose to power, becoming the *malik*, or king, of Egypt, where he proclaimed a return to Sunni Islam. By the 1170s, Saladin decided to pursue the higher goal of uniting all Muslim territories, including Syria, northern Mesopotamia, Palestine, and Egypt. His devotion to the idea of Muslim unification was further inspired by his commitment to jihad, or Islamic holy war, equivalent to the idea of a Christian Crusade. His final contribution to history was the civilized Muslim reconquest of Jerusalem in 1187.

This seventeenth-century woodcut captures a pensive Saladin. Although he spent most of his youth as a religious scholar, history largely remembers the Muslim ruler as a fierce opponent of the Christian Crusades.

Crusader Castles

Today, a series of Crusade fortresses remains along the Syrian and Lebanese coasts, including the castle of St. Louis in Sidon, Lebanon; Qalat Nejm and Qalat Rahba in Syria; and Nimrod's castle in the Golan Heights. The Krak des Chevaliers, still the most spectacular and one of the best preserved, sits on the Syrian-Lebanese border. Pharaoh's Island, a remarkable fortress that sits off the coast of the Sinai Peninsula, was built by King Baldwin I in the twelfth century and was later captured by Saladin.

Pictured here is the crusader fortress known as Krak des Chevaliers, which sits on the present-day border between Syria and Lebanon. Considered the best military fortress of the day, it was one of a chain of five other castles built to protect Homs (Emesa).

Zangi's son Nureddin succeeded him. From his capital at Aleppo, Nureddin worked to create one unified Muslim state. When he died in 1174, his lieutenant Saladin took power in Egypt and wrested Syria from Nureddin's eleven-year-old son.

During these battles, the Assassins, who had murdered numerous Muslim and Christian leaders, made two attempts on Saladin's life. The irate Saladin besieged their mountain fortress. Once trapped, they guaranteed Saladin his personal safety. Free of the Assassins' threat, Saladin returned his attention to repelling the crusaders.

Saladin drove the crusaders from every town in Syria and Palestine except for Antioch, Tripoli, and Tyre. In 1187, he took Tiberias. Saladin then laid siege to Jerusalem, which surrendered after one week. Saladin tore the Christian gong from the mosque and the golden cross from the Dome of the Rock. The crusaders were then forced onto a sliver of Syrian coast.

The Middle and Late Crusades

Saladin's victories enraged Christian Europe. England's Richard the Lionheart, Germany's Frederick

By 1140, the crusaders largely occupied the populated regions of the Levant, a region that became known as Outre-mer, a French word that means "overseas," because many of the crusaders thought of the region as a French colony. The Christian crusaders traveled overseas from France, or from European kingdoms controlled by the French, beginning in 1097. Within two hundred years, united Muslims reduced the Christian-controlled lands to a narrow strip of cities along the Mediterranean coast.

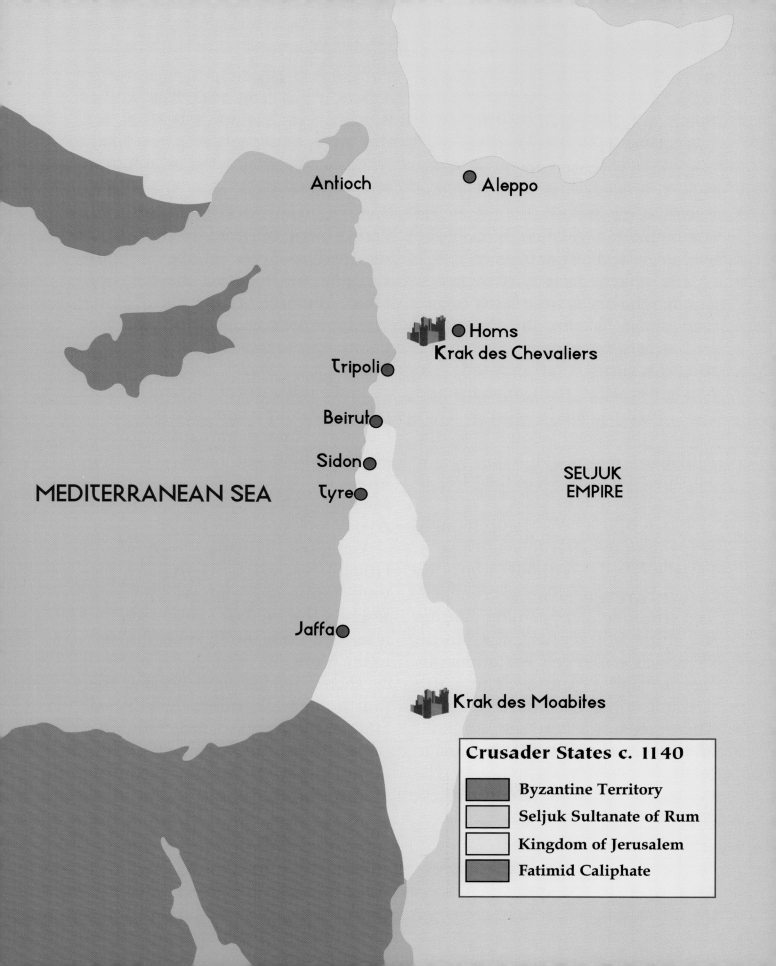

Antioch

Aleppo

Homs
Krak des Chevaliers

Tripoli

Beirut

Sidon

Tyre

MEDITERRANEAN SEA

SELJUK
EMPIRE

Jaffa

Krak des Moabites

Crusader States c. 1140

	Byzantine Territory
	Seljuk Sultanate of Rum
	Kingdom of Jerusalem
	Fatimid Caliphate

Barbarossa (who drowned before he reached the fighting), and France's Philip Augustus launched the Third Crusade of 1189 to 1192. They laid siege to the coastal town of Akka. Saladin rode in the next day and pitched camp opposite the enemy. He communicated with his opponents by swimmers and carrier pigeons.

The siege lasted two years. Though the Arabs were better organized under Saladin, the Europeans had superior weapons. Eventually, the Muslims surrendered. In November 1192, the Christians and the Muslims made peace. They agreed the coast belonged to the Christians and the interior to the Muslims. Pilgrims were then free to travel safely to holy sites.

Peace did not last long, though. A few months after this agreement, Saladin died. Without him, the Syrian-Egyptian sultanate crumbled. The crusaders kept coming. During the thirteenth century, the Fourth Crusade focused on Constantinople, Egypt, and Tunisia. The Fifth Crusade almost conquered Egypt. Then, tensions between England and France forced the Europeans to focus their energies at home. The tide began to turn. With the Sixth Crusade, Europe won Jerusalem in 1229 but lost it in 1244. The Arabs saw their opportunity. They drove the crusaders farther and farther from the Syrian heart of the Middle East. Imprisoned after the failed Sixth Crusade, King Louis IX of France was released in 1250. He returned to Syria on the Seventh Crusade and fortified the cities of Jaffa, Caerarea, Acre, and Sidon. The Eighth Crusade ended with the death of France's Louis IX in Tunisia.

In the last years of the Crusades, a new threat appeared in the East. Genghis Khan's Mongolian army was marching southwest. While the Mongols advanced, a Turkish Mamluk officer named Izz-al-Din Aybak took power in Egypt.

Genghis Khan's grandson Hülagü reached Syria in 1259. He took Damascus and Aleppo and reached the Mediterranean. Briefly, it seemed Syria and Egypt would fall to the Mongols.

Then Baybars, who became the fourth Mamluk ruler, demolished Hülagü's forces at Gaza, reuniting Syria and Egypt. Together, the kingdoms drove the Mongols from the Middle East.

6 THE OTTOMAN EMPIRE

Between 1516 and 1517, the Mamluks fell to the Ottoman Turks. This was a new Muslim empire based in Asia Minor. It had grown from Constantinople, which was the old capital of Byzantium and was now called Istanbul. The Ottomans were nomadic Muslim Turks from central Asia who had been converted to Islam by Umayyad conquerors during the eighth century. Led by Uthman, the third rightly guarded caliph, they founded a principality in 1300 amid the Mongol-wrecked Seljuk Empire in Turkey. The Western term "Ottoman" is derived from Uthman's name.

The Ottomans in Syria

In 1453, Mohammed II conquered Constantinople. His grandson Selim I — the Stern and Inflexible — expanded the borders created by his grandfather. He won a dramatic 1514 victory over the Shiite ruler of Persia. Next, Selim marched into Syria. Just north of Aleppo, in the Battle of Marj Dabiq, he crushed the Mamluks. A few months later, the Ottomans took Cairo.

Selim's successor was Süleyman the Magnificent. Under Süleyman, the Ottoman Empire stretched across North Africa to Algiers, Tunis, Tripoli, and Oran. When Süleyman died in 1566, the Ottoman

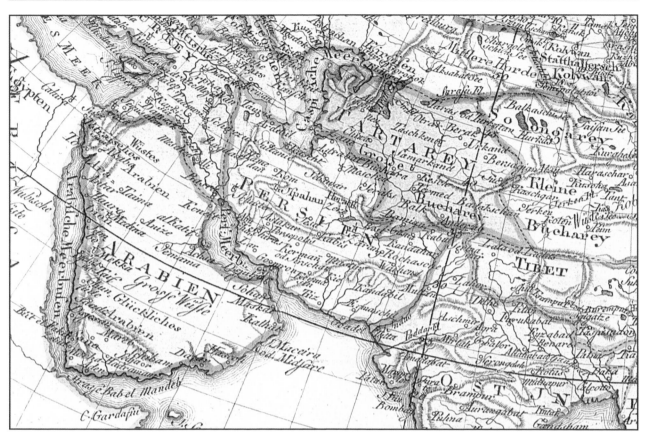

This eighteenth-century map of Asia, drawn in 1795 when the Ottoman Empire was in a state of steady decline, shows Turkish-controlled regions in the Middle East. The empire crumbled after a series of invasions, wars, and revolts. By 1882, the Turks had lost nearly 50 percent of their territory. Finally, in 1918, after the Turks lost World War I against the Entente Powers (France, Italy, England, and Russia), the once powerful empire collapsed. In 1920, Syrian lands fell under French rule.

Turks controlled the entire Arabic-speaking world except for Morocco, and the entire Sunni Muslim world except for parts of India. By the seventeenth century, the Ottomans had beaten back the Persians and absorbed Mesopotamia.

The Ottoman rise was not a total disadvantage for the Syrians. The average Syrian enjoyed more independence under the Turks than under the Mamluks. Religious minorities were freer to practice their beliefs because they accepted Arabic as the language of the Koran. Unfortunately, Syria needed a central government and the Turks did not provide one.

In order to manage their holdings, the Turks divided territories among governors. They carved western Syria into provinces around Aleppo, Damascus, Tripoli, and Sidon. In each province, a *pasha*, or administrative military leader, collected taxes, kept order, and ruled an area that was of little military significance. In rural areas, heads of important families took power. These provinces, or millets, were like tiny nations—a system convenient for the Ottomans, but one that splintered Syria and hurt its national unity.

The Decline of Ottoman Syria

Syria needed a government to rebuild its economy. Syrian trade had taken a severe hit in 1498 when the Portuguese sea captain Vasco da Gama sailed around the southern tip of Africa and opened a European sea route to India. European traders no longer needed to pass through the Middle East, an advantage for them that cost Syrian merchants and traders dearly.

Western trade with Persia continued to move through Aleppo, but, on the whole, it was diminished. Unlike the Mamluks, whose public works had included roads and rest houses, the Ottomans did not solve the problems that made trade difficult. Roads grew impassable, canals filled with silt, and robbers frequently attacked camel caravans.

Syrian industry had once been the source of some of the world's finest goods. During Mamluk rule, the skill of Syrian artisans was famous. Weaving, particularly, was a Syrian

This Venetian portrait of Süleyman I was painted during the height of Ottoman power. During the forty-six years Süleyman was in control (1520–1566), Ottoman territories doubled. Remembered as a legal reformer at the time known as the Ottoman renaissance, Süleyman was also a poet, honored by the Europeans with the moniker "the Magnificent."

specialty. Under the Ottomans, Syrian weavers continued to produce unusually fine cottons, wools, and silks, as well as the precious brocades, or damasks, so called because of their city of origin—Damascus. Between the sixteenth and eighteenth centuries, however, much of Syrian industry declined.

Many Syrians had tried and failed to fill the gap left by the failing industry with agriculture. There was some farmland in Syria, but a dry year meant fewer crops. Even worse, nomadic Arab tribes did not share the idea of private property. If their migration patterns led them across farmland, they simply pitched their tents and lived off the land.

By the end of the eighteenth century, every Arab province in the Ottoman Empire was in decline. As Ottoman rule weakened, tensions between Syria's Maronite Christians and a Muslim sect called the Druze grew violent. The Druze are a religious group living in modern Lebanon, Syria, Palestine, and Israel whose beliefs contain elements of both Shiite Islam and Christianity. In present-day Syria, the Druze are the third largest religious group.

In the nineteenth century, French Jesuits arrived in Syria to found schools for Maronite Christian children. Jesuits are Catholic missionaries who take a great interest in education. Concerned by the hostility of the Druze toward the

The rise of European imperialism contributed to the weakening of Turkish might, especially after fifteenth-century European explorers discovered sea routes to Asia. This discovery allowed Europeans greater access to exotic Asian goods at reduced costs. Not having to rely upon the slow delivery of goods by caravan, Europeans crushed Middle Eastern markets that no longer drew upon foreign merchants for endless taxes. Caravanserai, or caravan stations like the one shown in this contemporary photograph, quickly became obsolete.

This illustration depicts the massacre of Maronite Christians by the Druzes in the courtyard of a house in Bheir-El-Kamar, Syria. Escalating clashes between the two groups resulted in deadly violence by 1860.

Christians in the 1860s, France sent troops to Damascus to protect the Christians.

After some prodding, the Ottomans agreed to establish a Maronite region in Lebanon, making it an independent nation with a large Maronite population. France withdrew its soldiers from Syria. Without the French to protect them, the remaining Syrian Christians were attacked and massacred. In the time it took the Ottomans to restore order, 6,000 Christians were slaughtered.

7 TWENTIETH-CENTURY SYRIA

BLAC

REPUBL

CYPRUS
LEBANO
Beirut 192
PALESTINE

EGYPt

During the early twentieth century, Western (European and American) mission schools taught Syrians about nationalism and human rights. This education formed a generation that wanted freedom from the Turks.

During World War I (1914–1918), the British and French took up the cause for home rule of the countries of Syria, Lebanon, Palestine, and Iraq. After the war, the Meccan Emir Faisal challenged the Turks, leading an army reinforced with British troops and driving the Ottomans from Syria. In 1920, Faisal became the Syrian king.

Syria Under French Rule

What the Syrians did not know was that the French planned to occupy their country indefinitely. In May 1916, the United Kingdom and France secretly concluded the Sykes-Picot

Peace treaties such as those written at the Paris Peace Conference after World War I in 1919 helped determine the divisions of the remaining Ottoman Empire, which was divided between the French and British. Final divisions of the empire were determined by representatives from Great Britain, France, Italy, Greece, and Japan at the Conference of San Remo, Italy, the following year. The mandated territories were divided into three classes, according to their geographical location and economy, and were then assigned to individual powers. It was then decided that Iraq and Palestine would be governed by the British and Syria and Lebanon by the French.

Agreement, by which most of the Arab lands under Turkish rule were to be divided into British and French rule. The areas comprising present-day Syria and Lebanon were given to France, while Palestine and Jordan were assigned to the United Kingdom. Faisal refused to accept French rule. The French sacked Damascus and drove Faisal into exile. (He fled to Europe until 1921 when he was made king of Iraq.) For twenty-six years, until Syrian independence in 1946, the French ruled an angry Syrian population who felt bitterness against the West. Syrians were determined to reunite Arabs into one state, creating a sense of Arab nationalism.

Sheikh Taggadine *(above)*, the new president of independent Syria, inspects French troops outside the town hall in Damascus in 1941. Syria was granted independence when French general Catroux formally handed the country over in a nationally broadcast speech. British prime minister Winston Churchill explained British intentions regarding Syria: "We [sought] no British advantage in Syria. Our only [objective] in occupying the country has been to beat the Germans." The historic map *(right)* illustrates an Israeli attack on Syria in the 1950s. Israeli and Syrian forces battled near the Sea of Galilee *(arrow)* in one of the worst outbreaks of fighting since the end of the Palestine war. An Israeli spokesperson said Israeli forces killed fifty Syrian soldiers and captured thirty others in a massive retaliatory raid into Syria on December 12, 1955.

Regardless of their initial motives or actions, the French built roads, schools, and hospitals during this colonial period. They established a productive cotton industry and influenced administrative and government systems that are based on French models. Nevertheless, the Syrian memory of betrayal is still raw.

Even after World War II (1939–1945), when the French promised the Syrians independence, they remained powerful for another year. Syria's geographical position was very valuable to them. In March 1945, Syria became a charter member of the United Nations, which is an indication of its status as an independent nation. Finally, in 1946, the United States, the Soviet Union, and Britain forced France to withdraw. Syria then officially became the Syrian Arab Republic.

Syrian president Hafiz al-Assad (1930–2000), who led the country from 1971 to 2000, is remembered as an anti-Zionist whose diplomacy with Western countries was largely motivated by his desire for Syrian control of the Golan Heights. This 1987 photograph was taken in Kuwait City, Kuwait, during an Islamic summit meeting.

centuries. Creating a new regime meant reconciling the country's religious groups. The tiny Alawite and Druze communities were terrified the vast Sunni majority would smother them.

For twenty years, Syria was politically unstable. Between 1949 and 1954, it survived four military coups. In 1958, it formed a union with Egypt to found the United Arab Republic. It broke this off in 1961, when it realized that Egypt expected Syria to be a subordinate nation and not a partner. Another series of coups took place between 1961 and 1966. In 1963, the Ba'th party gained control. Hafiz al-Assad, who was a Sunni, was the military governor in Syria at the time and later became president of the Syrian Arab Republic.

Two French-educated teachers — a Greek Orthodox Christian and a Sunni Muslim — formed the Ba'th party in Damascus in the 1940s.

The Syrian Arab Republic

Syria found independence difficult. It had been under foreign rule for

"Ba'th" means "resurrection" in Arabic. In 1953, the Ba'th merged with the Arab Socialist Party. Its official name is the Arab Socialist Resurrection Party.

When Syria won its independence in 1946, it was an agricultural country, largely supported by cotton farming. Smaller plantations raised wheat, barley, sugar beets, tobacco, and sugarcane, which Europeans still loved to import. (Before that, European food was sweetened with honey.) Orchards produced olives, pomegranates, apples, apricots, almonds, and, along the coast, lemons and oranges.

In the 1970s, the Ba'th turned these private lands into state farms. It also took control of industry. As a socialist party, the Ba'th allied itself with the Soviet Union. Like the Soviets, Ba'th party members believed the government should control a nation's wealth. The Syrian government regulated textile production, food processing, and construction. It oversaw the mining of iron, manganese ores, rock salt, marble, and gypsum. Free enterprise, or the ability of citizens to enter into privately operated businesses, almost disappeared.

The Ba'th was very popular. Syrians liked its emphasis on Arab unity. They also liked its openness to members of all social classes. When the Ba'th rose to power, its ideas of social justice appealed particularly to Alawites. Many Alawites who joined were soldiers in the Syrian army, giving the party military might. Today, Alawites still dominate the Syrian officer corps, its police force, and its intelligence agency.

8 SYRIA, PRESENT AND FUTURE

In 1970, Lieutenant General Hafiz al-Assad led the military arm of the Ba'th to power in Syria. Assad was an Alawite and career soldier. He believed in a secular, or non-religious, Arab unity. Over time, he envisioned rebuilding a "Greater Syria" that would include Lebanon, Jordan, sections of Turkey, and Israel.

More than anything, Assad was determined to win back the Golan, or Syrian, Heights from Israel. The Golan is the rich, mountainous, southwestern corner of Syria. It provides an important strategic position for both Syrians and Israelis. During the Six-Day War of 1967, Syria, Lebanon, Jordan, and Egypt waged war on the nineteen-year-old state of Israel out of a conviction that the tiny Jewish nation had no right to exist in the Arab world. The Israelis repelled their attackers and seized the

Present-day Syria, as seen in this map, must face critical decisions for the betterment of its future. Peace talks with Israel over the return of the Golan Heights, the struggle with Turkey over the development of water treatment facilities for the shared Tigris and Euphrates Rivers, a sluggish economy, and the need for improved human rights are key issues facing the country in the new millennium.

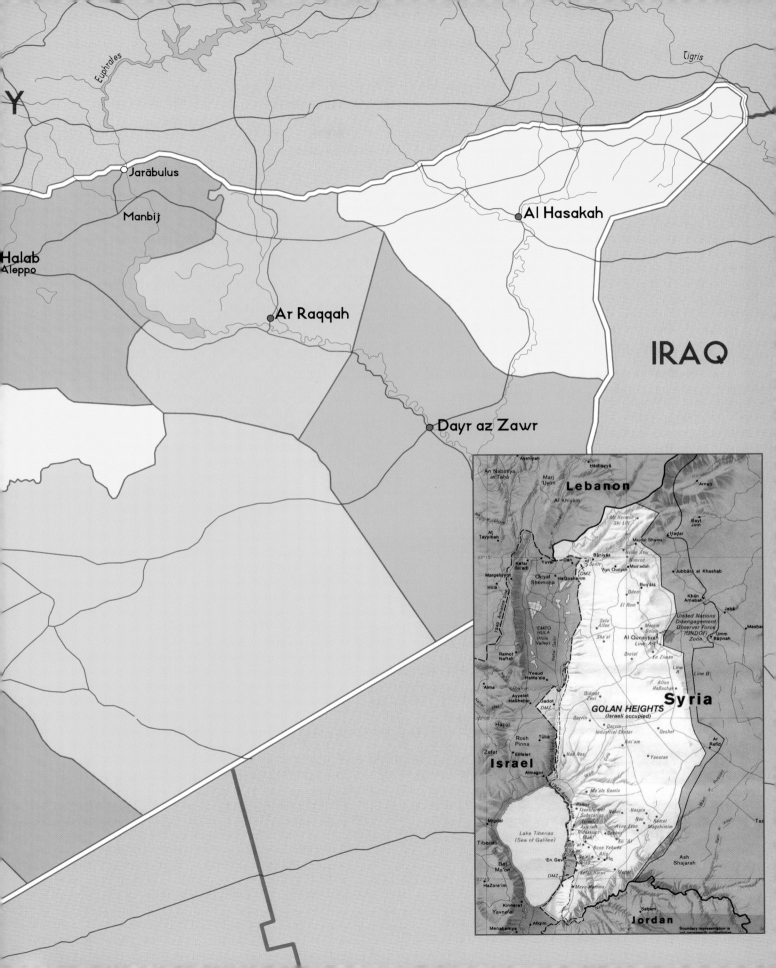

Golan Heights and continue to occupy the area today.

In 1971, after a bloodless coup, Assad was elected to a seven-year term as the Syrian president. Today, Syria is still a presidential republic. As president, Assad made policy decisions, appointed officials, and commanded the military. The first person in Syria's independent history to give the presidential office stability, Assad was reelected in 1978, 1985, and 1991.

Not all of Syria supported Assad and his Alawite government. During the 1970s, a radical Sunni organization called the Muslim Brotherhood fought to overturn Assad and the Alawites. Its members were mostly lower- or middle-class urban Sunnis who had suffered economically under Assad's leadership. Also, they believed Assad's ideas were Westernizing Syria because his policies neglected Islam. In addition, Assad kept his government in a constant state of military emergency, a condition that hurt civil liberties.

Muslim Brotherhood members believed that violence was the best weapon against Assad. In 1979 and 1980, bombs exploded nearly every week in front of government buildings. By 1981, the Brotherhood was implicated in 300 assassinations and had kidnapped Assad's personal interpreter. Assad responded by assassinating and kidnapping known and suspected members of the Brotherhood. He also sent armed Ba'th members into combat with Brothers. These skirmishes increased the level of violence in Syria, which, by then, was close to civil war.

Hama

Set 120 miles (193 kilometers) northwest of Damascus on the Orontes River, Hama is Syria's fourth-largest city. In 1980, a group of Hama activists issued a manifesto. They wanted Assad to honor the Human Rights Charter, end

This photograph of Israeli soldiers was taken on June 7, 1967, during the Six-Day War. The conflict between the combined Syrian, Lebanese, Jordanian, and Egyptian forces against Israel quickly became a demonstration of Israel's effective military forces. Before long, the Israelis repositioned themselves on the Sinai Peninsula, captured Jerusalem, and gained the Golan Heights.

Syrians display their national flag on April 17, 2001, in Ain Tineh, on the Syrian side of the Israeli-occupied Golan Heights, as they face the Druze village of Majdal Shams on Syrian National Day. Syria's outlawed Muslim Brotherhood called for Damascus to battle Israel on the Golan Heights, captured by Israel from Syria in the 1967 Arab-Israeli War, following the Israeli bombardment of a Syrian military position in Lebanon.

Syria's state of emergency, and hold free elections. If their demands were not met, they would strike against the government. These Hamawis were not Muslim Brothers. It was no secret to Assad, however, that the Brotherhood considered Hama their most important base for recruiting members.

In June of that same year, Assad was in Damascus. A group of Brotherhood assassins launched two hand grenades at him and let off a round of machine-gun fire. Assad kicked away one grenade. His bodyguards blocked the other. The next morning, Assad's soldiers entered the prison at Tadmur (Palmyra) and murdered between 600 and 1,000 Muslim Brotherhood prisoners. By 1981, street executions of people suspected of ties to the Brotherhood became common in Hama. Citizens frequently found bodies in the public squares after daybreak. The Brotherhood fought back with more bombings. Soon they infiltrated the air force and tried to topple the Syrian government.

By the following year, Assad had had enough. He sent 500 soldiers into the Barudi district of Hama on the western bank of the Orontes. They carried lists naming members of the Muslim Brotherhood slated for execution. As they advanced through the city, armed Brothers appeared on the rooftops and shot at them. Assad's men stumbled through the streets carrying their dead. Next, Assad sent in tanks. During a series of skirmishes, the Brothers held their own. Finally, the Syrian army stopped trying to target the Brothers. They simply burned the city to the ground. Army engineers dynamited buildings that remained standing in Brotherhood neighborhoods.

When the road from Damascus to Hama reopened in May 1982, it was possible to examine the destruction. Three large areas of the city had been razed. Crushed within these flattened fields of concrete were shops and apartment buildings full of people and their possessions.

According to Amnesty International, Assad's soldiers killed between 10,000 and 25,000 Syrians—mostly civilians—and left thousands more without homes.

The Future of Syria

Shortly before the crisis in Hama, during the mid-1970s, the Syrians struck oil. This radically changed their economy, giving the country the ability to provide its own fuel. In the 1980s, the Syrians discovered additional oil fields. They also located a natural gas source near Palmyra. As the economy improved, Assad loosened state control. Crops increased. Trade expanded. For the first time the Syrian government encouraged private business.

Life inside Syria improved, but its relationships with the outside world were strained. Atrocities such as the killings of the Muslim Brothers and innocent civilians that occurred in Hama angered countries concerned about human rights. Even worse, Syria, which continued to be hostile toward Israel and the West, was frequently linked to terrorist acts. Britain, for example,

The face of Syria has changed drastically since independence in 1946. Although the discovery of oil in the country boosted its overall economy, its growing population, demand for water supplies, and increased need for jobs have kept the economy from the growth expected from exporting large quantities of oil. Relations with neighboring countries such as Israel and Lebanon have remained tense, and Syrian forces have been stationed in Lebanon since 1976.

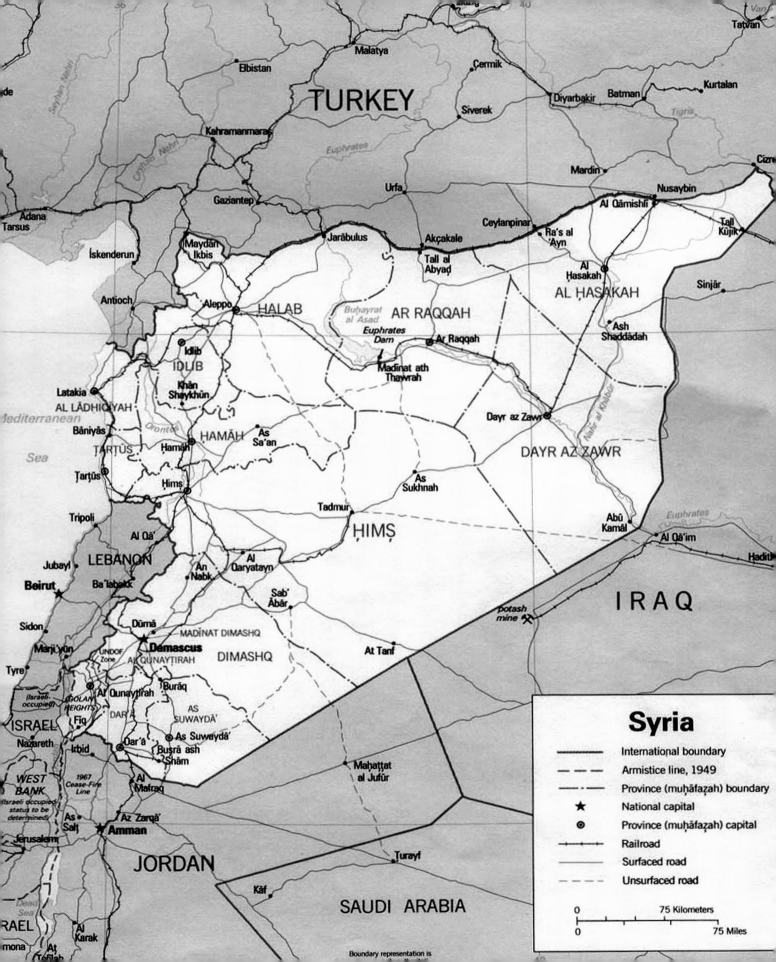

broke diplomatic ties with Syria entirely after the nation was accused of sponsoring an attempt to blow up an Israeli jet at a London airport.

For many years, Syria depended on the Soviet Union for military support. As the Soviet Union weakened during the 1980s, Syria needed new allies. Assad grew less isolated from the West. When Iraq's president Saddam Hussein seized Kuwait in August 1990, Assad joined an alliance that included France, Germany, the United

Syria's president Bashar Assad in 2002 during a summit of Arab leaders in the Middle East. Representatives of Arab lands agreed on a new stand toward Israel, offering peaceful relations for the return of so-called Arab land, a Palestinian state with Jerusalem as its capital, and a fair solution for Palestinian refugees.

States, Russia, and Egypt. At the end of the 1990s, Assad withdrew support from numerous terrorist organizations and began to repair relations with nations around the world. One of its greatest ongoing tensions was with Israel, which had occupied the Golan Heights since the Six-Day War of 1967.

On March 27, 2000, Assad met with United States president Bill Clinton. Clinton presented Israeli premier Ehud Barak's offer to withdraw from Lebanon. Barak also agreed to return Syrian access to the Sea of Galilee through the Golan Heights. But because this was a compromise—and not the full return of the Golan Heights—Assad did not accept.

After Assad's death in June 2000, his son Bashar took power. A younger son, Bashar was appointed when his older brother, Basil, died in a car crash. He had studied to be an eye doctor, not a politician, and was not an ambitious leader. A liberal contrast to his iron-fisted father, Bashar has inherited Assad's parliament, party, and popular support. Unfortunately, he lacks major international allies.

At the moment, Syria's allies are mainly Arab. It is a member of the League of Arab States, which includes Egypt, Iraq, Jordan, Kuwait, Lebanon, Palestine, Saudi Arabia, and much of North Africa. This is no guarantee of shared goals, however. Assad believed himself to be the only truly unifying force for the Arab world. Still, he was constantly at odds with Saddam Hussein's Iraq and with fundamentalist Islam. The desire for unity conflicted with each country's need for independence.

The Syrian future is unclear. In its infancy, Syria arose from between the giants of Egypt and Babylon. It survived the assaults and occupations of Rome, Byzantium, Turkey, and Europe. This vast history lives in its ruins and monuments. The fluted columns of Palmyra still stand, cracked and elegant, above arid Syrian sands. At Hama, twenty-first-century Syrians still listen to the groan of ancient Byzantine *norias*, or water-wheels, which raise water from the Orontes River.

This 1992 CIA map shows Israeli settlements in the Golan Heights. One of the most strategic territories in the Middle East, the Golan Heights has been an important area of occupation since 1948 when the region was first used as a base of military operations to launch attacks against Israel. The region was later captured by Israeli forces in 1967 during the Six-Day War, and Israelis continue to occupy the area today, though their position remains unofficial.

Today, Syria must carry the wisdom of its past into its future. It must balance an understanding of its role as a central Middle Eastern territory with its own needs and its place in the world.

TIMELINE

1200 BC Thousands of Minoan Philistines settle in Syria
334 BC Alexander the Great conquers Persia
323 BC Death of Alexander the Great
167 BC King Antiochus loots the Holy Temple of Jerusalem
63 BC Pompey advances on Jerusalem
272 Romans capture Palmyra
571 Muslim prophet Muhammad is born
613 Muhammad begins preaching the revelations
622 Muhammad moves to Yathrib; the start of the Muslim calendar
632 Muhammad dies
717 Arabs hold Sicily, Portugal, and most of Spain
750 Syria falls to the 'Abbasids at the Battle of the Zab
1095 Launch of the Crusades against Islam
1099 Christians capture Jerusalem
1169 Saladin takes power in Egypt
1187 Muslim reconquest of Jerusalem
1259 Genghis Khan's grandson, Hülagü, reaches Syria and takes Damascus
1914-1918 World War I
1916 United Kingdom and France secretly conclude the Sykes-Picot Agreement
1920 Faisal becomes the Syrian king
1945 Syria becomes a charter member of the United Nations
1946 Year of Syrian independence
1949–1954 Syria survives four military coups
1958 Syria forms a union with Egypt to found the United Arab Republic
1970 Hafiz al-Assad overthrows president Nur al-Din al-Atasi
1971 Assad is elected president of Syria for a seven-year term
1973 Syria and Egypt go to war with Israel to retake the Golan Heights
1974 Syria and Israel sign a disengagement agreement; Syria gains the Golan Heights
1975 Syria proposes peace treaty with Israel in return for Israeli withdrawal from Arab land
1976 Syrian army intervenes in the Lebanese civil war
1978 Camp David peace agreement between Egypt and Israel
1980 Muslim groups riot; a Muslim Brotherhood member tries to assassinate Assad
1981 Israel annexes the Golan Heights
1982 Muslim Brotherhood uprising in the city of Hama; Israel invades Lebanon
1983 Lebanon and Israel end hostilities; Assad suffers a heart attack
1984 Rifaat is promoted to the post of vice-president
1987 Assad sends troops back into Lebanon
1990 Iraqi invasion of Kuwait with Syria on U.S.-led coalition against Iraq
1991 Syria participates in the Middle East peace conference in Madrid, Spain
1994 Assad's son Basil is killed in a car accident
1998 Assad's brother Rifaat is 'relieved of his post' as vice-president
1999 Talks between Syria and Israel begin in the United States
2000 Syrian-Israeli talks postponed; Assad dies and is succeeded by his son Bashar
2001 Muslim Brotherhood resumes activity; Syria elected to UN Security Council
2003 After the U.S.-led victory in Iraq, U.S. secretary of state Colin L. Powell heads to Syria to discuss changes in the Middle East. The invasion of Iraq had been opposed by Syrian president Assad.

GLOSSARY

apostle A passionate supporter of a new cause or belief.

Assassin A member of a Muslim sect that secretly murdered its enemies, especially Christians, during the time of the Crusades.

brocade A thick, heavy decorative cloth that has a pattern of gold and silver threads.

caliph A civil and religious leader of a Muslim state.

convert To persuade to adopt a different belief, view, or party.

coup (coup d'état) A French term meaning "blow to the state" that refers to a sudden, unexpected overthrow of a government by outsiders.

exile To banish or expel from one's country or home.

hashish The flowering tops and leaves of the hemp plant that are used as a drug.

imam A prayer leader in a mosque.

incursion A hostile entrance into a territory; raid.

infidel Religious unbeliever.

Islam A religion based upon the teachings of the prophet Muhammad. Its followers, Muslims, believe in one god, Allah.

javelin A light spear thrown with the hand.

Koran The sacred text of Islam.

Mamluk A member of the Egyptian military class occupying the sultanate from 1250 to 1517; a white or east Asian slave in Muslim countries.

manifesto A written document that publicly declares the intentions, motives, or viewpoint of its issuer.

monotheism The belief that there is only one god, such as in the religions of Islam, Christianity, and Judaism.

mosque A building used for public worship by Muslims.

pasha A Turkish civil or military official.

raze To destroy to the ground.

secede To withdraw from membership in an organization or alliance.

sect A group that has separated from a main body of religious believers.

secular Not relating to religion.

Semite In modern usage, the term is linguistic: a Semite is one who speaks — or spoke — any of the Semitic family of languages: Akkadian (Assyro-Babylonian), Canaanite (Amoritic and Phoenician), Aramaic (Syriac), Hebrew, Arabic, and Ethiopic.

siege The surrounding and blockading of a town or fortress in order to capture it.

steppe A semiarid plain, often grass-covered.

sultanate A Muslim country ruled by a sultan, or king.

usurp To take possession without legal claim; to possess without right.

vassal Someone who receives protection from an overlord in return for loyalty.

vendetta Prolonged series of retaliatory, vengeful, or hostile acts or exchange of such acts.

FOR MORE INFORMATION

American-Arab Anti-Discrimination
  Committee
4201 Connecticut Avenue
Washington, DC 20008
(202) 244-2990
e-mail: adc@adc.org
Web site: http://www.adc.org

Center for Middle Eastern Studies
The University of Texas at Austin
1 University Station, #F9400
Austin, TX 78712-1193
(512) 471-3881

e-mail: cmes@menic.utexas.edu
Web site: http://menic.utexas.edu/
  menic

Web Sites

Due to the changing nature of Internet
link, the Rosen Publishing Group, Inc.,
has developed an online list of Web
sites related to the subject of this book.
The site is updated regularly. Please
use this link to access the list:

http://www.rosenlinks.com/liha/syria

FOR FURTHER READING

Ball, Warwick. *Syria: A Historical and
  Architectural Guide*. Northampton,
  MA: Interlink Publishing
  Group, 1997.
Burns, Ross. *Monuments of Syria: An
  Historical Guide*. London: Zed
  Books, 2000.
Davis, Scott C. *The Road from Damascus:
  A Journey Through Syria*. Portland,
  OR: Cune Press, 2001.

Morrison, John F. *Syria* (Creation of the
  Modern Middle East). Broomall, PA:
  Chelsea House Publishers, 2002.
Stark, Freya. *The Valleys of the Assassins*.
  New York: Modern Library, 2001.
Stoneman, Richard. *Palmyra and Its
  Empire: Zenobia's Revolt Against
  Rome*. Ann Arbor, MI: University of
  Michigan Press, 1995.

BIBLIOGRAPHY

Cohen, Aharon. *Israel and the Arab World*.
  Boston: Beacon Press, 1970.
Friedman, Thomas L. *From Beirut to
  Jerusalem*. New York: Anchor
  Books, 1990.
Hitti, Philip K. *History of the Arabs*.
  New York: Palgrave Global
  Publishing, 2002.
Hourani, Albert. *A History of the Arab
  Peoples*. Cambridge, MA: Harvard
  University Press, 1991.
Klengel, Horst. *Syria, 3000 to 300 B.C.:
  A Handbook of Political History*.
  Berlin: Akademie Verlag, 1992.

Landay, Jerry M. *Dome of the Rock*.
  New York: Newsweek Book
  Division, 1985.
Page, Jake. *Arid Lands* (Planet Earth).
  Alexandria, VA: Time-Life
  Books, 1984.
Spencer, William. *The Middle East* (Global
  Studies). Guilford, CT: Dushkin
  Publishing Group, 1992.
Toynbee, Arnold J. *A Study of History*.
  New York: Oxford University
  Press, 1946.

INDEX

About the Author

Allison Stark Draper is an author of many books for young people on historical subjects. She lives in upstate New York.

Acknowledgments

Special thanks to Karin van der Tak for her expert guidance regarding matters pertaining to the Middle East and Asia.

Photo Credits

Cover (map), pp. 1 (foreground), 4–5, 52–53 © 2002 Geoatlas; cover (background), pp. 1 (background), 6, 20, 28, 53 (inset), 57, 59 courtesy of the General Libraries, the University of Texas at Austin; cover (top left), p. 58 © AP/Wide World Photos; cover (bottom left), p. 10 (top) © Erich Lessing/Art Resource, NY; cover (bottom right), p. 43 © Ali Meyer/Corbis; pp. 8–9, 14–15, 16–17, 24, 30, 32, 36 (right), 39, 46–47 Maps designed by Tahara Hasan; pp. 9 (inset), 25, 42 © AKG London; pp. 10 (bottom), 11, 18 © AKG London/Erich Lessing; p. 16 (inset) © Corbis; pp. 17 (inset), 44 © David Halford 2002; pp. 19, 33, 38 © Sonia Halliday Photographs/Jane Taylor; pp. 22–23 © Stapleton Collection/Corbis; p. 36 (left) © Art Resource, NY; pp. 37, 48, 49 © Bettmann/Corbis; p. 45 © Corbis; p. 50 © Peter Turnley/Corbis; p. 54 © Vittoriano Rastelli/Corbis; p. 55 © AFP/Corbis.

Designer: Tahara Hasan; Editor: Joann Jovinelly; Photo Researcher: Elizabeth Loving